MORE THAN ANYTHING

NAICHE LIZZETTE PARKER

Copyright © 2018 Naiche Lizzette Parker
All rights reserved.

No part of this book may be reproduced in any written, electronic, recording, or photocopying without written permission of the publisher or author. The exception would be in the case of brief quotations embodied in the critical articles or reviews and pages.

This is a work of fiction. Names, characters, places, and incidents either are the products of the author's imagination or are used fictitiously.

Publisher: Crooked Queen Literature
ISBN: 978-1984314833

1. Poetry 2. Romance 3. Anthology 4. Fiction
First Edition

for me.

I love being in love. I've fallen for many people, places, and things in my twenty-two years, always purely and madly and rabidly. I'm sure there will be many more. For as long as I can remember, I've readily delivered myself over to the next muse, haven, or devil that's had its arms open. Loving that way over and over again has been a blessing and a curse.

Because of love, I've touched the moon, I've spoken to the stars, I've run away, I've found home. I've grown. I've felt brave and alive and unstoppable.

Because of love, I've memorized a map of hell. I've become possessed, exorcised out of lust. I've betrayed myself. I've made amends with myself.

And for all of it, I am grateful. For every single person who has made me feel this, I am grateful. For myself and this bravery to continue striking the match, I am grateful.

So here is my advice: Never turn your back on love. Feel every single gritty, explosive, agonizing, and beautiful bit of it. Love has begun and ended wars. Love has lived at the root of birth and death. It has made magic, electricity, miracles.

Those who claim heartlessness are not as strong as they seem. Those who have felt love at its most generous

and most ruthless and choose to open their hearts
again? An indescribable bravery.

So I continue to fall in love. I continue to pick roses
and bleed on the thorns. I continue to write love letters.

To everyone. To you, dear reader. To myself.

This is the longest one.

Sincerely,
NLP

I. IN LOVE

TEETH

i want to be
savagely in love.

i want even the wolves
to fear the things we do
beneath the full moon.

LOVE LIKE THIS

we exist in our own world,
the cigarette between your lips a smokescreen,
half-glances,
pauses for breath,
using moonlight as daylight,
your fingers morse-coding against my flesh,
the type of language my body
finally understands.

someone once told me,
"be careful with a love like this,
the kind that makes you forget
everything and everyone else,"

but i don't remember who.
i can't remember now.

LASTING

we do not make a habit of photographing the things we see everyday with the implication that we will always see them everyday for the rest of our lives, no photograph needed.

one afternoon, i advised myself to take a picture of every single thing i saw on my morning commute: the dying greens on my fire escape, the rat frying his breakfast on the train rails, the choppy waters of brooklyn bleeding into manhattan, atlas lugging the world on his shoulders alongside the rest of the businessmen near rockefeller center. i wanted out of this city. i wanted to start looking at things like it was the last couple of times.

but not you.

i know it hurts that i never photograph you.

i hope i never need to.

ECLIPSE

in this one,
the ghost of me lives on the moon,
translucent and blue-veined,
this solar-paneled garbage land;
the closest i can get to you.

in this one,
love is living in the eye of the storm
instead of dry land, for
i choose the small chance of living
above the small chance of living without you.

in this one,
i take your almost over
all of it with anyone else.

in this one,
i would spend eons in the dark
for a second in your light.

THE DEFINITION OF LOVE

everything i am afraid of,
you are feeding to me for breakfast.

there are ghosts in the apartment
that howl when you're gone.

for the first time,
i peel back the skin to bite down on the bone.

i don't want to sleep.
i never want to sleep.

FOUR IN THE MORNING

albany
the factories
the walmart parking lot
the rest stop
the coast;
you are caught in my pen cap,
you are all of my stories.

montauk in the winter,
that cemetery of snow,
the forest
the dead signal
the backseat of your car
popping a tire in a stranger's backyard;
always doing fearful things
to avoid fearing each other.

a playground
the devil's mountain
twin peaks;
you are an after-school special,
a french film,
i could have you in one sitting
but remember you for the rest of my life.

always midnight,
always neon,
always an empty road,
always the stars
always the junk food
and the wooden planks
and the fantasy.

we are fiction;
not even those asleep could dream us up.

you're pulling from me the things
i can't even allow myself to want.

WHAT IT WAS LIKE

i found a home inside of your adoration,
four walls of your chest,
pet names scurrying down the halls,
butterfly kisses batting their wings against the windows,
chandelier glint of your eyes.

i made a living out of loving you.

the moment you invited me in,
i was mesmerized.

CREATION

do you remember
when there were no countries?
do you remember the earth before
we sank our butter knives into it?

you came to me,
and i was divine.

i love you how a god must love.
building all this just to
give you something to break.

THE ENTIRE HISTORY OF US

you have awakened an ancient longing in me,
a want before my body was built,
a desire waiting patiently before the birth of my bones.

i have already loved you through
every witch burned at the stake,
every queen hanged by the neck,
every empress with her heart on the line –

i have lived in the light for eons
in anticipation of your eyes.

in each of these lives,
you are both the battle
and the armor.

when you kiss me,
i can taste tar and sand and wine
overflowing from the kingdoms
and country sides
and speakeasies that have already seen us fall together
and then fall apart.

wherever you kissed me then
is now a birthmark on this skin;
your fingers follow them like a timeline.

do you remember?
commandments were written
in fear of our kiss,
empires fell to make room
for what we have become.

i knew you were mine
when you held me and my body became
the vessel through which i could travel in time.
with you i have always existed and will always exist.

so come to me now.

touch me like we were gaia's sole intention,
like the whole universe formed just for
the potential of us.

unshackle me from the bind
of these years;
time has nothing on the way you calm
the revolt in me.

so come to me now,
and let us fix pangea's fate;
i am so tired of drifting apart.

these hearts of ours could find each other
through centuries
and wars,
across highways,
and from opposite stars.

ten light-years over,
after death,
eyes closed,
and in the dark.

CRUSH

i sent you five love letters
that never made it.
the mailman is fine,
but my courage isn't.

i. i saw you and became a mapmaker,
charting the path towards the parts of you
no one has yet touched.

ii. my ribcage is a prison
and these butterflies are restless,
desperate
for a place to migrate.

iii. your words drip like holy water;
every time we talk
i am born.

iv. ask anyone and they will tell you
that i don't have a green thumb.
i have killed every plant i've ever touched.
but to watch you bloom i'd raise every ocean,
scald my hands summoning the sun.

v. no myth can explain
what you've started in me.

WHEN A WITCH FALLS IN LOVE

when a witch falls in love,
the crows worry,
the moon is jealous,
the roses wilt.

you become the altar upon which
she lays all her blessings and
her curses,
summoning something immortal
from the parts of you
you'd laid to rest.

in her eyes, you are a match
striking against the book of her skin,
mouth spitting gasoline,
the feather of a phoenix,
the bite of a dragon,

unable to distinguish between the fire
that was already inside of her
and that which will be her end.

DREAMS

being a writer is visionary,
a writer infatuated is clairvoyant.
my heart has its hand on a pen,
always working on my love story
before it's even started.

i keep thinking about my person, somewhere out there.
i keep thinking about rough thumbs on my bottom lip,
peaches and leather, silver thistles and classic horror,
drive-ins and long stretches of road, the whole season
burning and things getting better, better, better.

they admonish me for this,
but when i choose you, i will be certain,
i will be ready,
the starting line will feel familiar,
the air horn will not startle us,
our engines will rev smoothly.

how powerful it is
to invent what you love
before it has the chance to love you.

in my arms
and under my pen,
you will never feel like a trick of the light
or an obligation of fate.
you will see me for the first time
and recognize me right away.

you are the chapter i penned with
my eyes open and hand steady.

i decided on you.
this affection is deliberate.

a soul mate is not a plot twist,
nor shooting star,
nor wishbone.

it is falling to your knees
and opening yourself up to what you invited in,
saying, "welcome home."

THE STRANGE WAYS WE REALIZE LOVE

i. he is still there when i close my eyes. all my life i was asleep until he asked me for the time.

ii. the morning i kissed her, the sunrise had a definition. i felt wrong and right and the whole sky opening above me, asking me who i was.

iii. names are just names until we adore the people who own them. yours has become a curse, a prayer, a song.

iv. i tell the officers to go home. there was no robbery here. i polished the jewels and delivered them myself. your hands were waiting, gentle. i am not a hostage, you are not pining for a better offer. i am willing and enough.

v. for the first time, i don't have to justify this to my heart.

SHE DOES LOVE YOU, BUT SHE'S TERRIFIED

you are a beast straight out of a children's book. you smile at her, and what she sees is wonderful and terrifying. your love looks like something she only recognizes from an old photograph or daydream.

in person, it grows claws, it makes magic, it has teeth.

she's burned her hand on the stove before, but this is a forest fire and she's in the middle of a hike she doesn't know the path of. she wants you to know that she's brave enough for this, but she needs a roadmap, needs a north star, needs something promising on the horizon.

because she does love you, but she's terrified. by the lavender and the pots and the window, she watches the village that survived the storms. the houses are broken through and thatched up, roofs still opening their mouths up for more water.

thirsty, but careful with what they have left.

you press her into the crescent moon, you make love to her against the stars. when you look at her that way, she calls it genesis. when you say the things you do, she opens up her wounds and hands you both a bandage and a knife. you decide.

she writes your middle name in ink above her hipbone.

she prolongs the bruise you left on her neck. she lets
out her heart when it's on a leash.

open, but leave your shoes at the door.

thirsty, but careful with what she has left.

THE ROAD

i want you like i want the gravel,
like i want the blur,
like i want one hundred miles per hour
straight into the dark.

you are an adrenaline lacking destination;

i don't know where we're going,
but i want to keep going.

SOMETHING LIKE IT

so few celebrate
the loves that were not quite love,
the people we use as plot devices,
the stars dotting the path towards
our true north.

the eyes that come with expiration dates,
glimpses of the way we will love fully someday,
one night, one month, one year,
one chapter before the climax of our hearts.

i am thankful for the preambles,
for the hands that have held my heart,
no matter how turbulent,
how careless,
for it is stronger with experience.

i used to feel like an excavation site,
dusted for handprints,
but now i know that we are walking museums
of habits and mannerisms and fondness
for the next person to adore
with all that we are filled with.

we don't have to see forever
when we look at each other,
sometimes we have to try
before we know how.

there is no finish line at the end of us,
but we're fine with
running in circles for now.

MORE DREAMS

we could just sit in bookstores and go upwards towards
the stars and find places to pick flowers and step on
each other's feet while soft music plays and run away to
the forest once a month and get lost in carnivals and
have a street musician that's our street musician and get
married in the mountains and read the same books and
just be nice to each other and nice to ourselves.

TELL HER NOW

tell her now,
while the tea is still boiling,
in the middle of the street,
with the trees leaning over to watch
and the lampposts flickering their eyes in surprise,
her bags packed with all of your second chances.

tell her now,
before the bombs burst,
before hades gets his hands on what you were,
before act two becomes a bloodbath,
before the crown gets its claws in your heart,
before the apple catches her eye,
before she leaves,
before you die.

by the time we see the stars above us,
they have already lived full lives.

somewhere in italy,
a man cannot decide what to pack for a train
that has already arrived.

tell her now,
if it is the last thing you say,
if it is the last mistake you make.

i would rather be blinded by the sun
than end with my eyes closed;
for it is never too late
until it is too late.

THANK YOU

we sit on the hood of your car,
and i lick the mango juice off your fingertips.
the sun paints us a deep orange;
the gas station shouts its neon right back.

you stand in between my legs with a toothpick
in your mouth,
and my dress rides up,
and my thighs are toasted red.

this is the most honest memory i have.

i cut my bottom lip on your family ring
and lick the blood off, too.
my cigarette singes
the hem of my dress.

i am the pretty portrait hanging over the mantle
that you've never looked at too closely
until the day that you do.

there is a wheel missing from
the bus trotting down the horizon.
there is a stroke of auburn
where the sky should be blue.

you squint at me
and my details finally come into focus.
you realize, i am not helen,
just the war.

but you don't run,

you bare your teeth
and brace for impact;
you do not hide it.

you give me what we are all looking for:
someone who loves us because of what we are
and not despite it.

YOURS, MINE

i once cried your tears,
once swallowed your pride,
once formed a bruise
in the place you have that scar.
i once fought your fight.

i once listened to the snake,
drank the cyanide.

this is what affection does to me:
i wear your shame just to
take it out of your body.

i become your mistakes
just to make them easier to forgive,
just to give them someplace to hide.

WISH UPON

why are we taught to fear
the beasts
and wolves
and witches
in fairytales?

would you not rather have me like this,
true with my intentions,
cursing you with my legs spread?
kissing you with my teeth bared?
loving you with my magic showing?

would you not cut me open with the glass slipper,
would you not eat the poison i have to offer,
would you not drown yourself to breathe like me?

APHRODITE

aphrodite lives in the desert,
in the lightning bolts,
in a rest stop,
in the gap between your teeth.

aphrodite lives in the motel room,
the butterscotch on your lip,
the bravery in the little boy thrusting a rose
at his kindergarten teacher.

aphrodite lives in that august haze,
the flush on your skin,
the dead weeks and the flickering carnival signs,
when everything is over and also just beginning.

aphrodite lives in the wrinkle of my mother's brow,
the chapstick between friends,
a box of chocolates,
the way you first mispronounced my name.

aphrodite lives in the cold coffee cup
and in between the strangers who both went to grab it,
the ghouls buried beside each other,
the girls watching boys by the sea.

aphrodite lives in this gum wrapper,
in your bent spine;
she set her sights on you
and decided to live in me.

THE BARROW GANG

this is not a nice story;
loving you is retribution
for the good girl i had to be.

i called you the devil
and you accepted the compliment.
i called you leviathan,
and we toasted to the sea.

this is gruesome,
but it is ours.
i understand now why we
revere ruins and swim out at high tide.

you came pockets empty
and filled them with the bits of me
you found small enough to fit inside.

you're the danger sign,
you're the edge.

you're the bottom of the bathtub,
the landing below the ledge.

i know that i chose this,
but here i am,
still flailing.

GRAVE ROBBER

i have died
over and over again.
some call this surviving.

i call this
the weight of
corpses.

i have died
over and over again.
you are a grave robber –

digging up the girls in me
i thought
i'd killed.

DRIZZLE

you whispered, "i'm always going to remember this."
the way the sky looked at us
and you looked at me,
the sound of the drums
in the orchestra of what we were together,
the stars, our pets,
begging us to name them,
the seismic waves you set off
inside of me,
the old woman who blessed us,
who cursed us,
"you two are going to be together forever."
the tides we forgot to pull in
because we were distracting the moon,
and even my morning toast tasted like you.

DOWNPOUR

i'm on the floor and you're gone
and i'm always going to fucking remember this.
the bus exhaust feels
like our last conversation,
i see your face in broken glass
and hear you mimicking the train conductor
every morning on the way to work
and laugh at our jokes
by myself,
like some monument to a battle
that no one is alive to know existed.

i bite my tongue,
and even the blood tastes like you.

II. OUT OF LOVE

THE RECKONING

i'm writing this to you
and the moon is begging me not to,
exhausted with collecting the bits of my broken heart
and guising them as stardust.

do you remember when we stopped at the side of
the road after driving hours into the night
to look up at the stars?

we were so small and
there were so many and
i wanted to tell you how endless this all felt then,
how infinite,
but i was afraid of handing myself over that way.

because i love you so much that my body
refuses to bend for anything else.
i love you so much that on forms
i start to write your name
as my home address.

this is the most fearful thing i have ever done;
i'm covering my eyes as if i didn't
pay for admission,
as if i wouldn't crawl into your woods
without a flashlight,
as if i wouldn't scale the grooves of your mountain
without even a rope to rescue me.

i picture us on the side of that same road
when we're eighty,
talking about this poem,

blessing the day we continued north,
sacrificing our youth to be infinite, too.

this can't be the universe where
we end up as the almost.
i can't die
as somebody you used to know.

MESSAGES ERASED

i. i miss you something terrible.
it feels like a bird has flown
out of my chest.

ii. one day
you will marry someone else
and i will marry someone else;
my biggest fear is that the memory of you
will show up to the wedding
without an invitation.

iii. california is on fire,
and i picked up the phone to talk to you about it,
but we're not each other's instincts anymore.
you're not my speed dial.
you're not my anything.

iv. you were more plane
than person:
flighty
and filled with emergency exits.

v. this was always the problem:
i love in a way that kills.
you love in a way that leaves.

ERASE (5) MESSAGES?

MESSAGES ERASED.

STITCHES

in the end,
you were a surgeon,
and i took the knife without going under.
this is how much i loved you:
i wanted to be awake for even
the awful bits of it.

in the end,
you were a surgeon,
whispering, "this is going to hurt,"
cutting me open
and forgetting
to sew me back together again.

MASOCHIST

i only know a love that hurts.

i have my hand on the stove,
my head in the lion's mouth,
your blade in my stomach,
whispering,
"thank you.
i was hungry."

i am the sword swallower's daughter;
taking your sharpness
and making a living,
mistaking all of this
for a gift

when you meant
for it to kill me.

PANDORA

i was pandora,
and you were ready to feel tempted,
coaxing the lid off with soft hands
and softer words.

you pulled from me
what i had kept in a closed box;

wanting to keep your hands warm by the fire,
but surprised when it burned.

wanting to build empires with the iron,
but frustrated when it wouldn't bend.

wanting to play in the dark,
then wreaking havoc when you couldn't see.

i was pandora and you took from me what you pleased,
detonating
and then blaming
the bomb.

all you left was hope,
and then you left me.

OUT

love is an assembly line
of things that come by,
incomplete,
i am
forcing broken parts to fit
where they shouldn't,
grabbing any piece i have
and jamming it into another
to give it a home.

when will i love someone
for a reason other
than their love for me?

i was raised a dreamer
upwards towards
my own destruction,
closing my eyes to everything we are,

sacrificing my heart
for everything i could turn us into,
everything we could be.

AFTER THE USING

the sheets are soaked
and i am crying;
inside and outside it's raining.

i am alice around a long table,
around some broken bottles;
you are getting bigger,
and i am getting smaller.

all i can think about is you, the funhouse,
needing your eyes to see myself.

all i can think about is how i have a catalogue
of backs without faces.

all i can think about is that love must be all this
but without punctuation.

FIXER UPPER

i watered the gardens,
i stocked the shelves,
i painted the walls,
filled them with laughter
and the smell of grass,
of wildflowers, of my perfume.

i tended to the bricks
when they fell from order.
i repaved every road that led in.

i drew open the curtains
and wrung them for dust,
i waited for the ceilings to stop leaking,
bucket in hand.
i hung up some paintings,
kept the roof sturdy,
stairs clean, windows open,
but closed when it rained.

i devoted my life, made it my pride,
poured love into the bannisters
and wood floors
and ashen hearths.

you told me you could never thank me enough
for all that i had done to turn
the house of your body
into a home.

you were finally ready
to move the next person in.

REMNANTS

after it was over,
i wanted to be nowhere.
i wanted to wipe the crime scene clean.

but i also wanted to be everywhere,
look for clues tucked in between our memories,
as if the pacific ocean could tell me
what you were seeing that day
when i thought you were looking at me.

SEPTEMBER

loss of love is devastation.
it is putting everything
you have ever owned
into the house of your dreams

and watching it burn
to the ground.

REFLECTION

i have begun to consider myself
a coffin.

this habit i have of opening myself up
and giving dead things
a place to rest.

WHEN THEY ASK ME ABOUT YOU

every person has a doctor frankenstein.
i came to you on ice,
clean for molding.
i came to you for the ripening.
i came to you for the programming.

you cut me open and
switched around my brain and heart.
there was blood.

(i was your peach)
there was bruising.

mary shelley told it best:
to me, you were god.
to you, i was body parts.

to this day, i am still writing you out of my code.
your voice still lives in the back of my throat.

CARNIVAL

it's not you,
it's us.

we were lions without tamers,
swallowing each other's fire,
jumping through hoops
just to see this through.

(come one, come all,
this man is going to pierce this woman
straight through the heart!)

convinced that it was time,
i sold my soul to the circus
without thinking.

the tent is down now;
i am up in a cloud.

it turns out that you
were just visiting.

THINGS THAT ARE WRONG WITH ME

i am the queen of hearts,
a heart of debts
with those who only
ever come collecting.

i'll let you live in me
(rent-free!),
always the one with beds to spare,
room to give,
extra to eat.

i am a magician at making myself
disappear in your presence,
dealing out second chances like playing cards
even though i already know
which one you'll choose.

i want to be kept so badly
that i'd hand my soul over to anyone
with room in the backseat.

i want to be loved so badly
that i'd drink the poison just to die full.

WINTER

the last time it was this cold,
you still loved me.

how awful it is to realize
that i can't skip the seasons
you don't live in anymore.

this becomes the story:
persephone returns from the earth
to find that hell is empty,
hades made chaos feel like home
then left her to live in it alone.

so she does what a woman must do:
rule the darkness he ran from.

so i do what a woman must do:
weather the storm and have faith in spring.

NOVEMBER

the last time i see you,
it's sundown and the coffee is cold,
my tongue is tired of this conversation.

fate has its pockets filled
with all the things
it's robbed from me.

THE WEEKEND FORECAST

i hate that i still check your horoscope
whenever i check mine.

i want to be your chance encounter
with an old ghost;
i want to be the door
that will be reopened;
i want to be the revisit,
rebirth,
regrowth you need when venus
passes through.

i still check your horoscope whenever i check mine,
and i hate it,
begging the stars to make room for me
in your fate.

WHEN FOREVER IS NOT FOREVER

i don't want to start over with somebody else;
i don't want to explain why i hesitate before the first
escalator step
or can't let my foods touch
or strip for eyes that don't remember
the tree we climbed to earn that scar on my hip.

i don't want a new nickname,
new set of goosebumps,
new pair of hands to feel safe in.

i took the time to read you,
i know all the words,
i know these lines,
i've memorized the map of your skin
and the path of your bones,
the peak of your smile –
i don't want to be the trail guide
for whoever will love you next.

my librarian,
you've been keeping all my stories.
how am i supposed to teach someone else
where the comedies are shelved?
where the tragedies hide?

i don't want to re-diagnose this heartache,
i don't have the strength to carry around another ghost.

i don't want to start over with anybody else.

LESSONS

i used to think,
right person, wrong time,
but is that true?

if you cannot love the seed,
do you deserve to watch it bloom?

ROME

i kept asking myself why.
why you left
why i hadn't
why we became what we did
why we cut the film before its ending.

and then i remembered a course i took
in college on why the roman empire fell.
we spent the entire semester trying to answer that
question and after neatly listing out every single piece of
research we'd obtained, every point in which one could
have salvaged the glory, my professor sat with our
papers in his lap, marked them all with a scarlet A, and
said something along the lines of,

"we ask ourselves why, but in the end, it still happened.
rome fell, and a new era blossomed from it. we wonder
about constantine, but we don't ache for him. we pose
for pictures in front of the ruins that were once on fire.
there were a million reasons why, and now there is only
acceptance. acceptance of what once was. acceptance of
what it is now.

have a good summer."

PRAYING ON DAISIES

it took me until after graduation
to realize that gatsby was not romantic.

i have been pouring my heart out like champagne;
everything ends facedown, mouth full of chlorine.

i have been throwing parties for
ghosts never in attendance.

when i peered more closely at the green light,
it was just a traffic sign.

AMEN

it's bittersweet,
this process of unknowing you.

the oddest things make me cry now:
neon diner signs in my periphery;
pictures of crescent moons;
winding roads;
3:03am;
any talk of the universe;
the sun showing its face after the first snow.

one day these things will just be
beacons of light,
prayer cards;
my new home;
a late hour;
on the tip of someone else's tongue;

something i used to love
with someone i used to know.

WOULD YOU DO ANYTHING FOR YOURSELF?

i was so proud of the way
i used to love him.

kept saying,
i would wait forever,
take whatever,
do anything
to be his.

i climbed the night sky and collected every star,
i waited in a dark room and went hungry for thirty days,
i swallowed the glass he left in my mouth,
i broke my bones to fit inside of him.

but he left anyway,
and i was once again alone with
my sister in the mirror:
cut fingers,
stomach empty,
bleeding lips,
broken bones,

begging,
"and what of
what you'd do for me?"

IT'LL BE LIGHT OUT SOON

losing him felt like forever –
but so must have
the first sunset
to those who didn't know
it would rise again.

ECHO AND NARCISSUS

1. the glass is:
   a. half-empty
   b. half-full
   c. a mirror

2. her eyes were:
   a. honey
   b. dill
   c. a mirror

3. the mirror:
   a. shows you what you are
   b. reminds you of what you are not
   c. all of the above

4. what did you see in her that terrified you?
   a. too much
   b. not enough
   c. yourself

TO WHOEVER WILL LOVE ME NEXT

i am too much.
i roar and out comes
the sound of
every person who's found a place
inside of me,
i am more inn than home
i play house
to even the people who were just visiting,
a guestbook of disappointments.
this poem is a mess
and i am a mess,
so every ending has been a mess.
when things shatter,
i am in such a scramble to fix myself,
i put back a few pieces
that were never mine.
there are so many people
i carry around on my back,
i'm sorry that i've given you
the burden of loving so many.
when you kiss me,
you might taste the cigarette
he was smoking when we said goodbye.
when you touch me,
you might feel the aftershock
of his earthquake.

THE VALLEY

there is a valley
between what we were
and who i am now;
i still vacation there.

i built a home
out of the walls you left
up around me,

painted
the color we picked out;
the art hung,
i bought on my own.

no one tells you that
the love migrates,
but the fondness won't fade.

to my skin,
you are an aftershock.
to my heart,
you are still a good friend.

i am learning to love you
in the past tense.

ACCEPTANCE

some people never grow up,
they only get older.

maybe this is both:

after two years i realized
that i cannot hate the plant
for growing after i stopped watering it
and someone else started.

i hope you are happy with her.

CATCHING UP

i love you,
but unbind me.

your first always
becomes folklore;
i have stuffed my cheeks with breadcrumbs,
desperate to leave you behind me.

i love you,
but untie me.

andromeda had a galaxy inside of her
but we remember her in chains;

i'm no good at necromancy.

we can't keep resurrecting this dead union
and pretending that it's fate.

my darling,
please release me.
let people see that i am more
than just the consequence of you.

i want to be a legend,
not a lesson,

the girl who knew how to leave,
good at goodbyes,
the girl who grew.

SOMEWHERE

how wonderful and
terrifying it is
that we will always exist
because we once existed,
we will always be here
because we were once here,
we will always be together
because we were once together.

somewhere,
a tree is still flaunting the tattoo
we gave it, our initials,
when we escaped into the mountains,
voice the sound of wind-kissed leaves,
whispering,
"they were here."

somewhere,
we are still driving along the salton sea
in an endless time loop,
just us and the road
and more road
pointing at the dead fish carcasses and empty shacks
where resorts used to stand proud and
children used to play,
and we are marveling at how
something that was once so alive
could be so empty now.

somewhere, we are still saying goodbye.

somewhere, we are still meeting for the first time.

YOU'VE CHANGED

i tried to be sweet.

you were a ventriloquist;
i tied strings to my wrists
every morning.
i tried to be your darling.

but you wanted me as a wolf
and then complained about the howling.
you wanted me as a diamond
and then refused my cut.

you left and it
left room for the devil
to climb inside of me.

now i'm the kind of storm
that knows its category.
i'm the kind of fire
that knows where it burns.

everyday you prayed for snow
and then hid from the blizzard.
don't raise hell
and then run from the flames.

WHERE IS THE GOOD IN GOODBYE?

they say that every time a tree falls,
the earth cries as if it's just lost an organ or
a limb, and it will tremble there from time to time.

(i guess i still shake in the places you left me,
like you are my phantom heart, still beating)

they say that loss is carrying around a pile of memories
you never got to make
and changing how this story ends
every minute of every lifetime i didn't spend with you.

(every night i ask the stars why
you took from me the part of myself that
you put there in the first place)

and oh, they say that grief is good.

(then without you i am golden)

IF

if i saw you again,
i would never tell you how much it hurt.
how much you killed me.
how long it took to yank the knife out.
that for sixty days,
i dined solely on memories
and let them eat me from the inside out.
that for sixty days,
i wept a river and
drowned twice
before i taught myself how to swim.

if i saw you again,
i would not show you the fire i breathe now
or
all the surviving i did
in your absence.

you don't thank the knife
for the skin that hardened
over the wound it made.

CAUSE AND EFFECT

i wish you could meet the person i became
because of you.

timelines are cruel that way.

SHOULD YOU

should you ever open the wrong photo album
and lock eyes with my plastic ghost,
or take a sip of champagne on your new anniversary
and suddenly taste my tongue;

i hope you don't rip it up,
i hope you don't spit it out.

i hope you remember that it did not rain everyday
where we lived,
that sometimes there was laughter,
that there were gifts we saved from the fire,
that when you wake her with a kiss,
it is a leftover meal from
the bowl of what used to make me smile,
that we saw things with each other
that we will never see for the first time with anyone else.

that most endings were once really good books,
and that, in drought,
we were once grateful for this storm.

that we were just two people loving
the best we could
with the hearts we had.

we were kind to each other once;
let's be kind to each other now.

in finding the courage to move away,
one must not burn the old house down.

TRY AGAIN

here's the thing. they break your heart, and you swear
you'll never be able to fall asleep next to anyone else
ever again.

and then one day it's 8am and you startle awake against
a new body you're calling home, a new set of eyes
you're calling forever.

that's the best part of all this, isn't it? how many times
we die before death.

the bravery it takes to throw ourselves at the things that
might resurrect us.

Naiche Lizzette Parker is a writer, witch, and lover of magic living in New York City. She was born with an abundance of words inside of her, and she's hoping to get them down on paper before her time is through.

naichelizzette.com

Printed in Great Britain
by Amazon